The Look-out

The Dead Man Files

Illustrated by Stephen Elford

With special thanks to our reader:
Mariyah Arif

First published in 2009 in Great Britain by
Barrington Stoke Ltd
18 Walker St, Edinburgh, EH3 7LP

www.barringtonstoke.co.uk

Title ISBN: 978-1-84299-715-4
Pack ISBN: 978-1-84299-789-5

Printed in Great Britain by The Charlesworth Group

TOP SECRET

Dead Man File

Name: Luke Smith

Age: 16

Cause of death: Car crash. Serious head and back injuries.

Date of case 6: November 2009

Mission: To stop a break-in and save a life ...

DMF

Contents

Intro

Luke Smith was killed in a car driven by his best mate, Joe. But that was not the end of it. Luke comes back as a ghost. What can he do to help people now he is dead?

Name:
Luke Smith
Age:
I6

Chapter 1

Now I am dead it is easy to travel about.
I watch over my family every day.

My gran lives in the country. There is a deep well at the end of her garden. Some days I stand by the well and watch her.

Name:
Luke Smith
Age:
16

Chapter 2

Jimmy Green and his mate, Zak, were the bad boys at school. I was in their class.

They went for old people because it was easy. The police had got them and they had done time for it.

By the garden gate, Jimmy and Zak spied on my gran. She was at the kitchen window and they were planning their move.

Jimmy told Zak that Gran was loaded with money. "It's in the house somewhere," he said.

Jimmy and Zak planned to rob her as soon as there was a night with no moon.

Name:
Luke Smith
Age:
16

Chapter 3

It was a dark night three days later. I was waiting by the well.

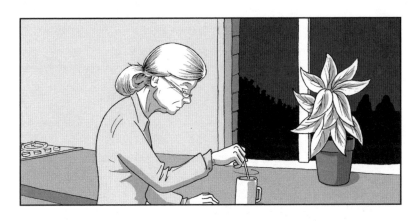

Jimmy and Zak stood at Gran's garden gate, looking into the kitchen window. She was by the sink, making herself a drink to take to bed.

They kicked her front door open. She looked round to see who it was. Then she fell over with the shock. Gran's heart was weak. Had she died of fright at seeing Jimmy and Zak in her house?

While Zak stole her rings and things from her bedroom, Jimmy found her hand bag in the hall and took her money.

Name:
Luke Smith
Age:
I6

Chapter 4

What do you do? Two rotten thugs are robbing your gran and she may be dying on the floor of a heart attack.

I used my powers to make the lights
flash on and off like crazy.

That stopped them.

"Jimmy, what's going on?" asked Zak,
hands full of Gran's stuff.

"Let's get out now," said Jimmy in a panic.

Name:
Luke Smith
Age:
16

Chapter 5

I stood behind the well at the end of the garden. I hooted at Jimmy and Zak as they came out of the house.

They came running after me like fools to see what was up. They jumped over the wall to get to me. But it wasn't the garden wall. It was the wall of my gran's well.

Down, down, down they went. I could hear them yelling all the way. Dull thump. Then it went silent.

Name:
Luke Smith
Age:
I6

Chapter 6

Inside the house I kept flashing the lights on and off until Bob Simms, a farmer who was going home late, saw them and stopped.

He saw the front door was smashed in.

"Are you OK?" he yelled to Gran.

No sound.

He went inside and found Gran lying on the floor. He phoned 999. The ambulance came.

Gran was saved.

THE DEAD MAN  FILES

Luke Smith is dead. But he's back to help those who need it ...

Watch out for more Dead Man Files coming soon ...

For more info check out our website:
www.barringtonstoke.co.uk